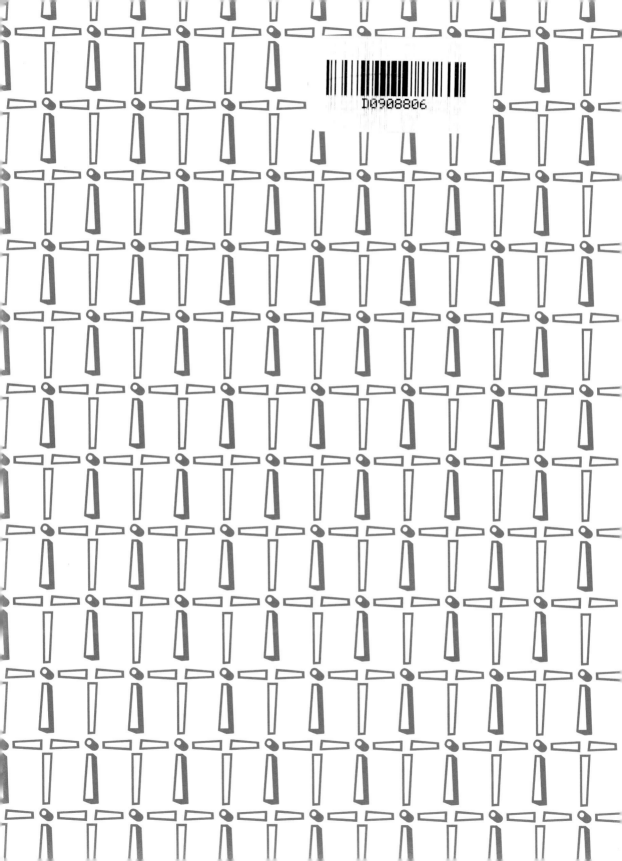

The Good Samaritan

AND OTHER BIBLE STORIES

BY REBECCA GLASER

ILLUSTRATED BY BILL FERENC AND EMMA TRITHART

SPARK
HOUSE
FAMILY

MINNEAPOLIS

Contents

Book design by Toolbox Studios, Dave Wheeler, Alisha Lofgren, Janelle Markgren, and Ivy Palmer Skrade
Illustrations by Bill Ferenc and Emma Trithart

24 23 22 21 20 19 18 17 16 15   1 2 3 4 5 6 7 8 9 10

Library of Congress Cataloging-in-Publication Data

Glaser, Rebecca Stromstad, author.
  The Good Samaritan and other Bible stories / by Rebecca Glaser; illustrated by Bill Ferenc and Emma Trithart.
      pages cm. — (Holy Moly Bible storybooks)
  Summary: "Illustrated retellings of several popular parables from the Bible." — Provided by publisher.
  Audience: Ages 5-8
  Audience: K to grade 3
  ISBN 978-1-5064-0251-2 (alk. paper)
1. Jesus Christ—Parables—Juvenile literature. 2. Good Samaritan (Parable)—Juvenile literature. 3. Prodigal son (Parable)—Juvenile literature. 4. Bible stories, English—Gospels—Juvenile literature. I. Ferenc, Bill, illustrator. II. Trithart, Emma, illustrator. III. Title.
  BT376.G53 2015
  226.8—dc23
                           2015020851

Printed on acid-free paper

Printed in U.S.A.

V63474; 9781506402512; OCT2015

The Parable of the House on the Rock

Jesus loved to teach people about God by telling parables. Parables are stories about everyday things, like planting or building, and everyday people, like parents and kids!

One day, Jesus told a parable about two builders to teach about faith.

Two men each set out to build a home. The first man climbed up a tall rock. Stomp, stomp! He pounded his foot on the big, strong rock. "I'll build right here on this sturdy foundation!" he said.

Thump thump! Clink clank!

He got to work building his house.

Draw where you would build your home.

4

The second man wriggled his toes in the soft sand. He didn't want to climb up a big rock. "I'll build my house here on this warm sand," he said. He quickly built his house, then rested in the sun.

Clouds filled the sky, and with a *trickle* and a **drip**, it started to rain. A great **smack** of thunder cracked across the sky. The first man hurried into his house, where it was safe from the storm.

The second man scurried inside too, but the rain and wind knocked his house down!

Just like the man on the rock, God's people should build their faith on a sturdy foundation— God's Word. When we hear and listen to God, our faith becomes strong!

The Parable of the Sower

Jesus told a parable about planting, or sowing, seeds to teach people about listening to God.

A sower's job must be easy, right? Just plant the seeds in the ground. But seeds need lots of things, like sunshine and water and, especially, good soil.

A sower went out to sow one day, scattering and flinging seeds far and wide. Each little seed found its own place to land.

Plink, plunk!

Some of the seeds landed on the smooth path. **Swoosh!** A flock of birds flew down and ate up all those seeds.

The seeds on the path are like a person who hears God but doesn't understand. When we don't understand, we quickly forget!

Some of the seeds landed on rocky ground. **Pop!** They sprouted up quickly but died in the hot sun.

The seeds on rocky ground are like people who listen to God when they're happy but forget God when they're unhappy.

Some of the seeds landed among thorny bushes. **Squish!** The weeds choked the new plants, and they died.

The seeds in the thorns are like people who worry too much and forget to listen to God.

13

Other seeds fell on good soil. **Grrrrrow!** The plants grew up strong and healthy and made more seeds!

The seeds in good soil are like people who listen to and understand God. They tell everyone about God's word, spreading God's love far and wide.

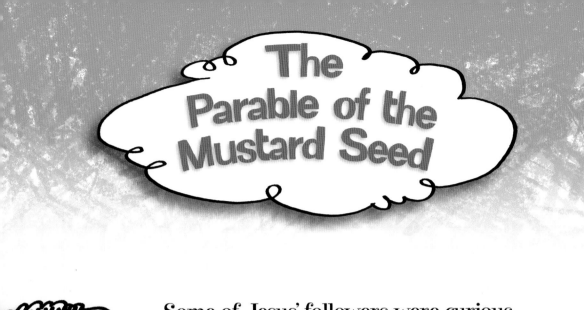

The Parable of the Mustard Seed

Some of Jesus' followers were curious. "What is the kingdom of God like?" they wondered. Jesus helped them understand by telling a parable about a mustard seed.

A mustard seed is tiny! Color the seeds.

The kingdom of God is like a mustard seed. It starts out tiny. But when it's planted, it grows into a HUGE mustard tree.

The big mustard tree has lots of room on its branches for birds to nest in its shade.

The kingdom of God has room for ALL God's people to live and be safe.

The Parable of the Good Samaritan

People knew they should love their neighbors, but many Jewish people and Samaritans did NOT like each other. So Jesus told a parable to teach about neighbors.

A Jewish man walked along the road to Jericho. Suddenly, a group of robbers attacked him. They hurt him, stole his money, and left him lying by the side of the road.

A priest walked along the road toward the hurt man. The man called out for help, but the priest looked the other direction.

"He's not my neighbor. No time to stop!" the priest thought as he hurried away.

Soon, the man saw a woman and her son coming near. But the woman reacted just like the priest.

"He's not my neighbor. I'd better keep going!" she thought as she rushed away.

Another person was walking toward the man. Oh, no! A Samaritan! The man worried that the Samaritan would hurt him too. But the Samaritan knelt down next to the man and helped him up.

"You're my neighbor. I'll bandage your wounds and find you a safe place to rest," the Samaritan said.

The Samaritan brought the hurt man to an inn and paid the innkeeper to care for him until he was healed.

23

Neighbors help people in need—not just their family and friends. The Samaritan man helped the Jewish man, even though Samaritans and Jewish people didn't like each other. Jesus taught that we should all be neighbors to each other—even people we don't like!

The Parable of the Prodigal Son

Jesus told a parable about two sons and their father to help people understand God's love.

A father had two sons. The younger son dreamed of going on an adventure. "Father," he asked, "can I have my inheritance early, so I can travel far away?"

The father agreed and gave the younger son his inheritance. A few days later, the son set out on his journey.

In a faraway country, the younger son spent his inheritance on parties and clothes and expensive food.

The older son stayed home and worked hard for his father. He plowed and cleaned and cared for the animals.

27

After a short time, the younger brother ran out of money. He took a job feeding pigs, but he realized the pigs had better food than he did! He was muddy and miserable.

Draw how you would feel if you were the older brother.

28

The son missed his home and his family, but he knew he didn't deserve to go back. "Maybe my father will let me be his servant," he thought. He decided to go home.

When his son arrived home, the father was filled with joy. "Welcome home!" he cheered.

The older son was NOT joyful. "Why are you happy to see him?" he complained.

"I thought your brother was lost, but now he is found," the father explained. "Let's celebrate!"

More Activities

LOOK AND FIND

Find the big rock in The Parable of the House on the Rock.

The wise man built his house on a solid rock. Much of the rock in Judea is limestone.

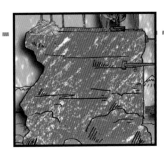

Find the  in The Parable of the Sower on pages 9–14.

These seeds were probably wheat or barley. They stood for the ministry that Jesus was planting in the world.

Count the birds in the mustard tree on page 18.

The area where Jesus preached has one of the largest and most diverse bird populations in the world.

Find the people avoiding the hurt man on pages 20–21.

The man was hurt on a road called the "Bloody Pass." Passersby may have been scared of being attacked if they stopped to help.

Find the  from the Parable of the Prodigal Son on pages 25–30.

Pigs were considered unclean animals under Jewish law.

ACTION PRAYER

Dear God,

Your kingdom is bigger, *(open arms up wide)*

Your kingdom is closer, *(bring hands to chest)*

Your kingdom is more amazing *(wave hands in the air)*

Than we can imagine. *(open and close hands on sides of head)*

Thank you for sending Jesus to show us what the Kingdom of God is like.

Amen!

MATCHING GAME

Match the person from the Bible with the fact about them.

1. I paid two denarii to an innkeeper to help my Jewish neighbor. Each denarius is worth a day's wages.

2. I asked for my father's money and spent it all quickly.

3. I plant by scattering seeds in a field.

4. I built my house on sand. I stand for people who hear but don't act on Jesus' teachings.

5. I told many parables, short stories that helped to teach a lesson.

6. I built my house on a rock. I stand for people who hear and try to follow Jesus' words.

7. I was a Jewish man who was attacked on a road called the "Bloody Pass."

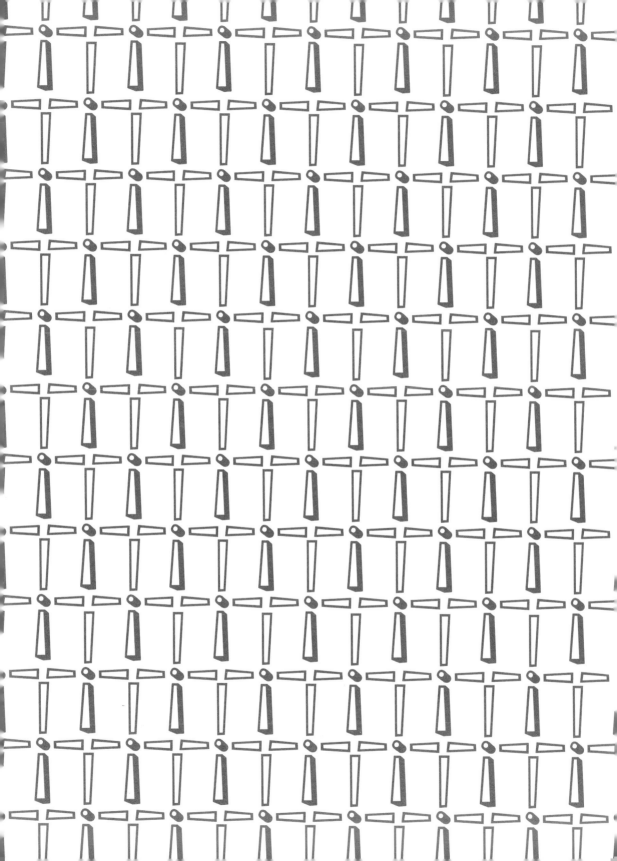